SEVEN ANIMAL STORIES FOR CHILDREN

RETOLD BY HOWARD I. BOGOT AND MARY K. BOGOT
ILLUSTRATED BY HARRY ARATEN

PITSPOPANY

New York · Jerusalem

Published by Pitspopany Press
Text copyright © 1997 Howard I. Bogot and Mary K. Bogot
Illustrations copyright © 1997 by Harry Araten

Design: Stephanie and Ruti Design

PITSPOPANY PRESS books may be purchased for educational or
special sales by contacting: Marketing Director, Pitspopany Press,
40 East 78th Street, New York, New York 10021 Fax: (212) 472-6253

ISBN: 0-943706-40-8 Cloth
ISBN: 0-943706-41-6 Softcover

Printed in Hungary

DEDICATION

From the Authors

Honoring the memory of
MAXINE LIVINGSTON ELBAUM (z"l)
and the friendship of RUBY and SIDNEY D. LEADER, M.D.

From the Illustrator

For Nittai
with love from his grandfather

CONTENTS

"Croak! Croak! Croak!"

Everyone speaks to God in his or her own way.

At the end of an especially rough day, King Saul would ask his favorite musician, David, to play the harp for him. David's beautiful music always calmed his nerves.

One morning King Saul was awakened by a wonderful song of praise that David was singing to God. As he heard the beautiful words, the king had an idea.

He called for his servants and said, "A king should make his subjects happy. So, proclaim to everyone that tonight there will be a special concert in the royal gardens, with a special guest singer."

That evening the royal gardens were so filled with people that many had to stand. Some climbed into the royal trees, hoping to get a glimpse of the surprise singer.

The king himself announced his surprise.

"Many of you may not have heard young David at the harp, but his praises to God are so beautiful that I want all the people to hear them."

David played the harp and sang his songs to God. At the end of the concert, people stood up and clapped loudly, asking for more. The king took David's hand and held it up high. Everyone shouted and yelled for joy.

After the guests left, David stayed in the garden with a few friends to play some of his favorite melodies. Suddenly, David's music was interrupted by a loud, "CROAK, CROAK, CROAK."

"What is that awful noise?" David asked.

Everyone looked around but couldn't find where the noise was coming from. As he started to play again, David's song was once more interrupted by the loud croaking noise. David was very upset. Could someone be playing a trick on him?

"We must find what or who is making that awful noise," he told his friends. Everyone started looking around the garden.

"I've found the noisemaker!" shouted Jonathan, the king's son. Everyone came running to Jonathan, who was by the side of a pond. He pointed to a very large frog sitting on a lily pad in the middle of the pond.

The frog liked having an audience and sang out with great joy, "CROAK, CRO-OAK!"

"Stop that terrible noise," David commanded the frog. "You are interrupting my songs of praise to God." David was certain the frog would jump back into the pond and swim away. But, much to his surprise, the frog jumped up onto a large rock right next to him.

"CROAK, CROAK, CROAK!" sang the frog.

"Stop your awful croaking this second!" David shouted again. "Can't you see you're ruining my beautiful songs of praise to God?"

The frog looked up at David and cleared its throat. "CROAK, sir," the frog said, "my CROAKing might sound terrible to you, but

I'm sure God likes my CROAKs of praise as much as your songs of praise. After all, you have your way of singing and I have mine."

David was shocked. But then he realized that what the frog said was true.

Then he began to smile. He leaned down and gently placed the frog on his palm, stroking its back. He turned to his friends and said, "Today I have learned a great lesson, one that I shall never forget. The frog is right. Every person and every creature has a special way of praising God, and God loves all their songs."

With a final "CROAK!" the frog jumped off David's palm, and back into the pond.

THINKING THOUGHTS

1. What was wrong with the way David spoke to the frog?

2. Why is it important to show respect to other people?

3. How do you show respect to your parents and teachers?

The Canary's Sweet Song

Sometimes just asking for something you want is not enough. You have to deserve it, too.

"Everyone quiet!" howled the North Wind, blowing a mighty sandstorm across the desert.

The eagle, the bear, the peacock, and the canary stopped talking and calmed down.

"As you know," the swirling North Wind continued, "the Jewish people have been chosen to receive God's Laws. They are to teach God's Laws to all the peoples of the world. And these Laws are to be given on a special mountain in the land of Israel. I have been asked to choose that special mountain.

"That's why you were all summoned -- to tell me why the mountain you live on is so special."

All four animals were excited. Each wanted their mountain to be chosen as the special place where God's Laws would be given.

"Begin," the North Wind commanded them.

The eagle, from Mount High and Mighty, spoke first:

"My mountain is the highest mountain in the land of Israel. Certainly God's Laws should be given on the mountain that is closest to God. From the peak of my mountain I can fly high up into the heavens or I can swoop down on any animal and catch my dinner," the eagle squawked, looking hungrily at the canary.

Then the bear began to brag about his mountain, Mount Big and Bold:

"My mountain may not be as high as the eagle's mountain, but it's much bigger. All the Jewish people could fit snugly on just one side of my mountain. Surely God's Laws should be given on such a wonderful place. And, it's got plenty of caves for me to hibernate in during the winter," the bear growled.

The peacock, from Mount Beautiful and Proud, spoke next:

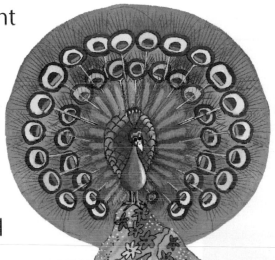

"How can you compare my mountain with those other mountains? Look at the beautiful flowers and flowing streams on my mountain. God's Laws should be given on a lovely mountain. Tell me the truth, have you ever seen such colors?" the peacock boasted, suddenly spreading his feathers for all to see.

Now it was the canary's turn. She was perched on Mount Sinai. After a moment, she began to sing:

> *My mountain is not high*
> *Nor big nor bold.*
> *My mountain is not proud,*
> *Nor beautiful to behold.*

> *My mountain is pretty small,*
> *Not important at all.*
> *But it suits me just fine,*
> *I'm happy, because it's mine.*

The bear growled. The eagle squawked. The peacock fanned his feathers. All three were very happy. They were sure the canary's mountain would not be picked. It was not great at all, not nearly as great as their mountains.

The North Wind whistled and blew across the sky. His thunderous voice could be heard all through the land of Israel. Finally, with a big BOOOM! he swooshed down to earth.

"Here is my decision," billowed the North

Wind. "The Jewish people, although small in number, have a big job to do. God's Laws teach that you shouldn't be too high and mighty nor too bold nor too proud to help others. God's Laws teach that you should be happy with what you have in life.

"So it is only right that God's Laws should be given on a mountain that is not too big or too proud or too mighty. God's Laws should be given on Mount Sinai!"

And that very day the Jewish people stood at the foot of Mount Sinai and received God's Laws.

THINKING THOUGHTS

1. *What do you think are some of God's Laws?*
2. *Why do you think the mountains of the eagle, bear, and peacock weren't chosen?*
3. *A modest person doesn't go around telling everyone how great he or she is. In what way was the canary modest?*

A Snake On Trial

When someone does something nice for you, it's important to say "thank you."

Many years ago, in the city of Jerusalem, there lived a wise and gentle animal doctor named Dr. Kalev. He loved animals so much that when an animal was in pain, he felt the pain, too.

One cold winter evening, as he was walking home from his animal hospital, Dr. Kalev heard a faint hissing sound. He followed the sound to a big tree. There, curled up around the tree trunk, was a very long, rainbow-colored snake. Dr. Kalev noticed at once that the snake was shivering and crying large tears.

Dr. Kalev bent down and patted the snake on the head. "What's wrong?" he asked. "I'm a doctor. Perhaps I can help you."

"I haven't been able to find any good food for several days and I'm so hungry," sobbed the snake. "Now it's gotten so cold, I'm sure I'm going to die."

"Don't be afraid," Dr. Kalev replied. "You're not going to die. I can help you. You wait right here."

Dr. Kalev ran back to his office and quickly warmed some milk and poured it into a bottle. Then he hurried back to the tree and fed the shivering snake.

"That was yummy," said the snake happily, when he had finished the milk, "but what I would really like is to crawl under your coat. It looks so warm and I'm still shivering."

"Why certainly," agreed Dr. Kalev. But no sooner had the snake coiled itself inside his warm coat, than it began to squeeze the good doctor. "Ouch! You're hurting me," Dr. Kalev gasped. "Why are you squeezing me so tightly?"

"Listen, Doc," the snake hissed, his forked tongue flickering near the doctor's neck. "You think milk is enough for a big snake like me? I need to eat something juicy and alive. Like you! That's the way snakes like me behave. That's our nature."

The doctor pleaded with the snake, "Please, don't squeeze me anymore. You are killing me. Didn't I just save your life?" But the snake refused to let go.

Then, Dr. Kalev had an idea that might save his own life. "Well how do you know it's your nature? Maybe you're wrong," gasped the doctor. "Only one person knows the nature of things. That's King Solomon."

"I've heard of him," said the snake. "He knows everything. And he's fair. Okay, we'll let him decide."

King Solomon listened carefully to what the snake and the doctor had to say. Then he said, "Snake, in order for a judgment to be made, both of you must be equal. Therefore, since the doctor is standing on the ground, you will have to uncoil yourself and stand on the ground too."

The snake obeyed. But no sooner had he reached the ground, than Dr. Kalev quickly put his boot on the snake's head, holding him tightly in place.

"Ouch! Have mercy!" the snake begged.

Pointing his finger at the snake, King Solomon spoke in a stern voice.

"After the way you tricked the good doctor, I should advise him to kill you. You were selfish and cruel when you had a chance to return a kindness done to you. Unfortunately, that's your nature. So since you can't help being what you are, I won't have you killed. Instead, I am sending you away. Don't ever show your face here again. Now go!"

Without even a hiss, the snake wriggled out from under Dr. Kalev's boot and slithered away.

THINKING THOUGHTS

1. What did the snake do wrong?
2. Why is it important to help animals whenever we can?
3. Besides saying "thank you," what are some other ways to show gratitude?

Spiders Make Good Friends

A friend is someone who's on your side, even when it's not the popular thing to do.

One afternoon, David, the Royal Harpist, was practicing a new melody on his harp. He was eager to play it for the king and he wanted to get it just right.

Suddenly, a furry purple spider dropped down on a thread right in front of David's nose. "Hi, my name is Weaver," said the spider. Then he pointed to a spot near the ceiling. "We're neighbors. I live up there in that corner of your room. I love listening to you play your harp. I'm your biggest fan."

David and Weaver became friends. While David played his harp, Weaver would spin his webs. And as David raced his fingers across his harp, Weaver criss-crossed his web, spinning and spinning long silver strands.

"Weaver," David would tease, "you spin the threads of your web almost as fast as I pluck the strings of my harp."

"Even faster," Weaver would answer, hanging from a thread.

Not long after, David learned that the king had become angry with him.

"He's jealous because everyone likes you more than they like him," explained the king's son. "If I were you, I'd leave the palace, quickly."

That night, David ran away from the palace. When the king discovered that David had run away, he saddled his horse, gathered his soldiers, and raced after him.

David wandered far and wide, looking for a safe place to hide from the king. After many days he found a cave. When he started to clear away the thick web that covered the entrance to the cave, a little voice shouted, "David, please be careful! You're ruining the web I use for my summer vacations."

"Weaver! Am I happy to see a friendly face," David sighed with relief when he spotted his friend. "The king and his soldiers are chasing me. I need to hide in this cave, but I doubt they'll be fooled for long. As soon as they come in and search the cave, they'll find me and throw me in jail."

"David," Weaver said, "don't be afraid. You rest now. When you wake up from your nap, you'll see that I've made our cave a very safe hiding place."

David was awakened by the sound of the king's guards approaching on horseback. "Listen, they're coming," David whispered to the spider. David was really scared. There was no way out of the cave except the way he had come in.

"I'm a prisoner in my own hiding place," he thought to himself.

"Your Majesty, we've found a cave," one of the soldiers announced.

"Good," the king replied. "David must be hiding in there. Let me through. I want to catch him myself."

David held his breath. He heard the king walking toward the cave. Then it was very quiet. David was sure the king would suddenly appear and shout, "I've got you!" But instead he heard the king shout at his soldiers.

"You've made a mistake. David can't be in this cave. Just look at this thick spider's web. Clearly, nobody's been in this cave for a long time. Let's look someplace else."

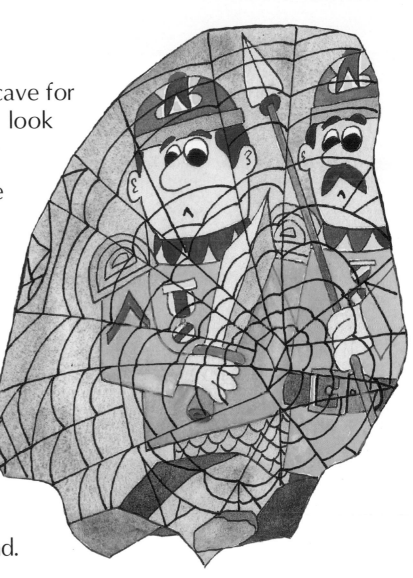

Sure enough, while David was sleeping, Weaver had quickly re-spun the thick web that David had destroyed when he entered the cave. Thus Weaver had saved David from the king and his soldiers.

"Okay, I admit it," David said to his friend. "You're the fastest!"

"I know," Weaver smiled.

THINKING THOUGHTS

1. How did Weaver help his friend, David?

2. Why do friends like to do things for each other?

3. What was the nicest thing you ever did for a friend?

A Whale Of A Tale

When you have a job to do, don't think up excuses to get out of doing it.

Jonah lived many, many years ago in Israel. His job was to tell people how God wanted them to behave.

"Stop acting like those terrible people of Ninveh," he would tell the Jewish people. "Do God's commandments."

But the Jewish people wouldn't listen to him.

Then one day, Jonah received a message from God.

"Jonah, the people of Ninveh are stealing, cheating, and being cruel to each other. You must go to Ninveh at once and tell them to stop their terrible behavior or the whole city will be destroyed."

"Don't send me, please," Jonah said to God. "What if the people of Ninveh actually listen to me? What if they start behaving nicely toward each other? How will it look if the terrible people of Ninveh listen to me, but the Jewish people don't?

You'll want to punish the Jewish people for not listening to me, won't you? And it will be all my fault!"

God did not answer, yet Jonah knew he was expected to go. But instead, that very night, Jonah ran away. He boarded a boat sailing in the opposite direction from Ninveh.

"Let God send someone else to Ninveh," Jonah said to himself. "I don't want to be the cause of bad things happening to the Jewish people."

But Jonah soon discovered that he could not run away from his job as a messenger of God.

A storm appeared out of nowhere, rocking and shaking the boat. The sailors on the boat shouted, "What have we done? We're sinking! We're sinking!" Jonah saw that the storm was only over his boat. The sea was calm everywhere else.

"It is not you who have done anything. It is I who have done something wrong," he announced. Then Jonah jumped into the water and the storm stopped.

The sea began to swirl around him. Suddenly, a whale appeared and swallowed Jonah. Jonah tumbled onto the tongue of the whale, flipped down the whale's throat, and landed in the whale's stomach.

"I'm alive," he cried as he picked himself up. Fish were flopping all around him. "But how do I get out of here?"

"It's up to you," the whale said. "You have to decide when you are ready to leave."

Jonah thought for a moment, and then he finally understood. "God saved me because I'm supposed to finish my job. I am a messenger of God and I must deliver my message. Is that right?"

The big fish answered by burping Jonah onto the shore, only a short walk from Ninveh. Jonah got up, brushed himself off, and walked into the center of the city.

Jonah went right up to the king's palace and knocked on the door.

"Where did you come from?" asked the king's guard.

"Just tell the king I have an important message from God," Jonah told him.

The king himself came to see the messenger of God. And when Jonah told him what God had said, the king announced, "This is truly a messenger of God. We must all listen to him. Everyone must act nicely to each other. No more fighting. No more cheating. No more lying. We must be good!"

Like their king, the people of Ninveh accepted God's commands. They listened to Jonah and their lives were changed.

Jonah went back to the Jewish people. Now, he told them, "Start acting like those good people of Ninveh. Do God's commandments."

And so they did.

THINKING THOUGHTS

1. What kind of things do you think God tells his messengers?
2. How do you think the lives of the people of Ninveh changed after they listened to Jonah?
3. What's the hardest job you have to do?

The Raven And The Dove

When you feel good about what you are doing then the chances are excellent you will succeed.

oah was a wise and kind person. But those around him were very mean and wouldn't help each other or tell the truth or even care for a little puppy, even if it came right up to their door.

God saw all this and was very upset.

"Noah," God said, "I am going to send a flood that will wash away all the terrible people in the world. I want you to build a big boat and take your family and many of the animals onto the boat. When the flood comes I want everyone on the boat to be safe."

Noah listened to God and built a boat called an Ark. It was like a floating hotel and a giant zoo put together.

Of course, Noah's friends and neighbors laughed at him.

"Where are you going to put all those animals?" they teased.

"Stop being such a worry wart. There's not going to be any flood," they assured him.

But Noah paid no attention to them.

Just as the Ark was finished, it started to rain. "Hurry," Noah said to his sons, "help me with the animals, then get on board."

By the time Noah had guided the last of the animals into the Ark, rain poured down in sheets of water. The Ark started to float.

Inside the Ark, everyone was trying to help each other. It was crowded and smelly and the rain made everyone miserable. But only the raven complained.

"What a terrible day. Won't this rain ever stop? When will we see land? I want some fresh worms. It's too crowded. I need to stretch my wings."

When the rain stopped, Noah said, "The raven is so eager to stretch his wings, I think we should grant his wish. Let's see if he can find fresh food and dry land."

Noah was surprised when the raven said, "Why me? Why should I do anyone a favor? And besides, how do I know someone won't steal my perch while I'm gone?"

But Noah opened the window and sent the raven out. The raven tried to get back in, but Noah pushed him back out again and again. Finally, the raven flew away. He flew and flew until he spotted a bush full of berries, sticking out of the water. This was a sign that the waters were going down!

But the raven was no longer thinking about signs or returning to the Ark. He began to eat the berries. He ate and ate until he was ready to burst. Then he settled into the bush and went to sleep.

Meanwhile, everyone on the Ark waited and waited and waited. Noah turned to the dove. "I don't know what happened to the raven. You must look for dry land."

The dove replied, "I'll be happy to go." But the first time she flew out she couldn't find dry land. The second time, however, she spotted an olive tree. The dove bit off a branch of the olive tree and carried it back to Noah.

"Hooray! Hooray!" Noah's family cheered, clapped, and jumped up and down. The animals barked, chirped, growled, snorted, meowed, clucked, trumpeted, hissed, quacked, and howled for joy.

The raven awoke and, having eaten all the berries, flew back to the Ark. All he could think about was, "I wonder who's sitting on my perch."

THINKING THOUGHTS

1. *Why did the dove want to do what Noah asked and the raven did not?*
2. *What kind of attitude do you think the people of Noah's time had?*
3. *How can you tell if a person has a good attitude or a bad attitude?*

The Royal Bee Kiss

Don't be afraid to say "I'm sorry," especially if you did something wrong by accident.

Once upon a time, in the ancient land of Israel, King Solomon was taking a royal nap in his royal garden. He was sleeping so soundly that he couldn't hear the buzz of a small black and yellow bee flying above his forehead.

"Buzz, buzz," buzzed the bee. "My name's Betsy. You're King Solomon, aren't you?"

When King Solomon didn't reply, Betsy landed on the king's nose, hoping to get a closer look at the king. She absolutely loved his kingly face, especially his kingly nose.

"Ouch!" roared the king, suddenly no longer asleep. "What's happened to my nose? It feels all swollen."

Betsy was so scared she flew away as fast as she could.

The king stormed back to the palace. He called his wise men and asked them why his nose had become so red and  swollen.

One wise man suggested, "Maybe you're allergic to one of the royal desserts, Your Majesty."

Another said, "Perhaps you should change your royal soap."

Yet another wise man offered, "I'll bet some evil magician has put a nose curse on you, Your Majesty."

But King Solomon was not happy with the advice of his wise men. So he left the palace and headed toward the royal zoo. Perhaps one of the animals might have a clue.

All the animals came to stare at the king's nose.

The monkey chattered, "What a big nose you have."

The elephant trumpeted angrily, "What's wrong with a big nose?"

The hyena took one look at the king's nose and began to laugh hysterically. "Hee ha haw hee! It's clear to me that your nose hurts because you were stung by a bee!"

"A bee? How do you know it was a bee?" asked the king.

"Ha! I have seen many bee stings," the hyena chuckled. "But if you don't believe me, hee hee, ask the Queen Bee."

Immediately, the king had the Queen Bee summoned to the palace. "Did one of your subjects do this?" King Solomon asked, pointing to his nose.

The Queen Bee buzzed close to the king's nose and announced, "I'm afraid so, Your Majesty."

"Find the bee that did this and bring her to me!" the king demanded. Without a word, the Queen Bee buzzed off. Minutes later she returned, with Betsy trailing behind her.

"Did you do this?" King Solomon asked Betsy. Betsy flew close to the king's face, but not as close as the first time.

"Yes, Your Majesty," Betsy admitted. "But please don't be angry with me. I was flying through your garden when I saw you sleeping. I had always heard what a wise and wonderful king you are and I couldn't resist giving you a special royal bee kiss."

"A royal kiss?" mumbled the king. "Well I suppose that is a good reason. A very good reason. As a matter of fact, you are a very brave bee, and an honest one, too.

"I'll tell you what, little bee. I will make you my personal royal bee and you can fly in my royal garden any time you wish. But I have one favor to ask of you."

"Ask me anything, Your Majesty," Betsy buzzed with joy.

"Next time you feel like kissing me, just give me a hug instead!"

THINKING THOUGHTS

1. Why wasn't the king angry at Betsy?
2. What's the difference between a bee's hug and kiss and your hug and kiss?
3. If you were Betsy, how would you have answered the king?

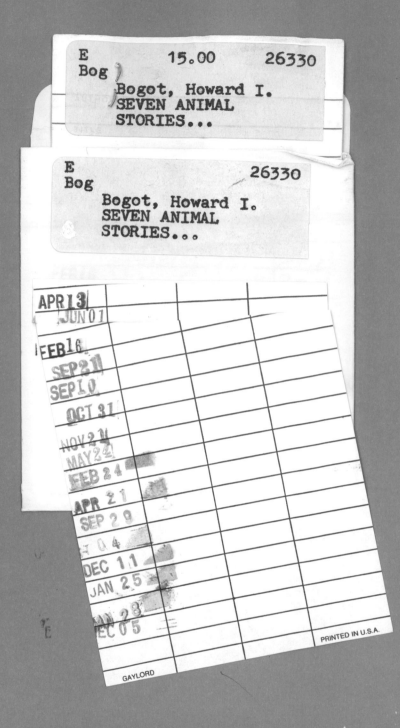